Original title:
Seasons of Marriage

Copyright © 2024 Swan Charm
All rights reserved.

Author: Liisi Lendorav
ISBN HARDBACK: 978-9916-89-286-2
ISBN PAPERBACK: 978-9916-89-287-9
ISBN EBOOK: 978-9916-89-288-6

Shifting Landscapes

Mountains rise with silent grace,
Cloaked in mist, they leave no trace.
Rivers carve the ancient stone,
Whispers of a world alone.

Fields of gold bend in the breeze,
Nature sways with effortless ease.
Clouds cast shadows, soft and light,
Day gives way to gentle night.

Forests hum with hidden sounds,
Life abounds in tangled grounds.
Leaves tell tales of seasons past,
In this realm, nothing can last.

Deserts stretch with endless sand,
Silent beauty, vast and grand.
Stars emerge in velvet skies,
Dreams awaken with their rise.

Oceans dance with vibrant waves,
Secrets held in hidden caves.
Tides that ebb, then flow again,
Nature's loop, a timeless chain.

Dappled Light

Soft hues dance on the ground,
Whispers of the leafy crown.
Sunlight filters through the trees,
Creating art with gentle breeze.

Patterns shift as shadows play,
In this place where light holds sway.
A moment caught, a fleeting sight,
Nature's canvas, pure delight.

Nurtured Roots

Deep within, they intertwine,
Silent strength, a bond divine.
Through the earth, they draw their might,
Grounded firmly, out of sight.

Leaves above reach for the sky,
Branches stretch and seem to fly.
But it's below, where life ignites,
Nurtured roots claim their rights.

Fragments of Forever

Moments caught in timeless frames,
Echos whisper love's sweet names.
In the heart, those memories glow,
Fragments of what we used to know.

Pieces stitched with laughter's thread,
Words of kindness gently said.
Though seasons change and years may roam,
In our hearts, they find a home.

Raindrops on our Journey

Each drop, a story falling down,
Washing paths in nature's gown.
Together we walk, hand in hand,
Amidst the storm, we take our stand.

Puddles form, reflecting skies,
With every splash, our spirits rise.
The journey flows with every storm,
United, we find our warm.

Moments Like Leaves

Moments fall softly, like leaves in the breeze,
Drifting in silence, they dance with such ease.
Whispers of time, in colors they show,
Each moment a treasure, as seasons will flow.

Captured in stillness, they shimmer and glow,
Memories linger, in heartbeats they grow.
Fleeting and fragile, yet deeply they weave,
Our stories, like branches, beguile and believe.

Antique Gallop

Hooves echo softly on cobblestone streets,
A tale of the past in each rhythm it beats.
Worn leather and brass, with stories untold,
Galloping forward, through memories old.

Winds from the ages whisper secrets anew,
Echoes of laughter, adventures they drew.
Antique carriages roll through the mist,
Reminders of moments that time can't resist.

Moonlit Vows

Under the moon's gaze, where shadows entwine,
Two souls make promises, their hearts now align.
Stars bear witness to the secrets they share,
Entwined in the magic, they float in the air.

Soft whispers linger, like silken caress,
Promises rooted in love's sweet finesse.
Bathed in silver light, their dreams take flight,
Moonlit vows echo through the cool of the night.

Serenity in Change

Gentle the tides as they shift with the moon,
Seasons of life, like a soft lullaby tune.
Branches sway lightly, their dance is so pure,
In change, there's a beauty that welcomes the sure.

Leaves fall to the ground, yet they're part of the tree,
Embracing the cycles, we learn to be free.
Each ending a start, a new story to write,
In serenity's arms, we find our own light.

Radiance of Yesterday

In the glow of fading light,
Memories dance in soft delight.
Whispers of the sun's embrace,
Time's warmth leaves a gentle trace.

Shadows stretch across the field,
Moments lost, yet never sealed.
Each heartbeat, a tale to share,
Radiant truths beyond compare.

Threads of Connection

In the fabric of our dreams,
We weave thoughts like gentle streams.
Each thread a bond, both strong and true,
Connecting hearts in all we do.

Through laughter, tears, we intertwine,
In moments shared, our spirits shine.
With every touch and every glance,
We find our love in life's grand dance.

The Harvest Moon

Golden light adorns the night,
Fields aglow, a wondrous sight.
Underneath the giant sphere,
Dreams of bounty feel so near.

We gather 'round, our hearts align,
In gratitude, our souls entwine.
The harvest brings a hopeful tune,
Guided by the watchful moon.

Flickers of Affection

In the dark, a soft spark glows,
Tiny flames that warmth bestows.
Each flicker tells a story sweet,
Of love that makes our lives complete.

With gentle sighs and fleeting touches,
Our hearts ignite, as passion rushes.
In every glance, in every sigh,
Flickers dance – we dare to fly.

Rituals of Reflection

In quiet dawns, the world awakes,
With gentle whispers, the heart shakes.
Thoughts like shadows dance in sight,
Seeking solace in morning's light.

Moments captured, echoes stay,
In stillness, we find our way.
Each breath a memory left behind,
In the spaces, peace we find.

Beneath the surface, waters flow,
Depths of feeling we come to know.
In silent rituals, we unearth,
The hidden paths of our own worth.

With every leaf that turns and falls,
Nature's wisdom softly calls.
Time reflects in each small hour,
As branches bend beneath the flower.

In starry skies, our dreams take flight,
Every wish a guiding light.
Through rituals, we learn to see,
The beauty of our mystery.

Moments Like Changing Leaves

Like leaves that shift from green to gold,
Moments pass, their stories told.
In shades of crimson, life unfolds,
Whispers of autumn in the cold.

Each breeze recalls a laughter shared,
Time shifts softly, never spared.
With every season, lessons grow,
A tapestry of life in flow.

Golden sunsets, shadows cast,
Moments linger, fleeting fast.
In every glance, a memory gleams,
As life unfolds in vibrant dreams.

Like the rustling of the trees,
We gather strength in gentle ease.
Let each change bring clarity,
As we embrace our destiny.

With every dawn, new colors bloom,
Chasing away the hint of gloom.
Moments like leaves, they drift and sway,
Teaching us to seize the day.

Starlit Memories

Underneath the endless sky,
Where starlit whispers softly lie,
Each twinkle holds a tale of old,
In their glow, our dreams unfold.

Moments captured in night's embrace,
Silent echoes through time and space.
The constellations, maps of fate,
Guiding hearts as we create.

In midnight hours, we sit and stare,
Finding solace in the air.
Each star a spark of hope's sweet light,
Guiding us through the darkest night.

Memories dance in moonlit beams,
Casting shadows on our dreams.
In every glimmer, warmth resides,
Where love and longing gently bides.

As dawn approaches, stars will fade,
But in our hearts, the memories stayed.
Starlit moments, forever bright,
A tapestry of love and light.

Symphony of the Elements

In whispers of the wind we hear,
Nature's song, both calm and clear.
From mountains high to valleys deep,
A symphony of life we keep.

Water's flow, a gentle grace,
Reflects the skies, a mirrored face.
In every ripple, stories flow,
The essence of life's ebb and go.

The fiery sun ignites the day,
With golden rays that dance and play.
Each warmth brings forth the blooms anew,
Life awakening in vibrant hue.

Earth beneath, steadfast and strong,
Holds the roots where we belong.
In its embrace, we find our place,
A harmony in nature's grace.

As elements entwine and weave,
We learn to cherish, love, believe.
In every note, a life expressed,
In nature's song, our souls are blessed.

Interlaced Paths

Two lives entwined, a dance of fate,
Through winding roads, they hesitate.
In silent whispers, secrets shared,
A bond unbroken, hearts laid bare.

Footsteps echo, in moonlit glow,
Together they walk, with hopes to sow.
In tangled branches, stories bloom,
Each turn they take dispels the gloom.

A journey forged in laughter bright,
Through darkest clouds, they find the light.
With every step, their dreams align,
Two souls, one path, in love they shine.

Twilight's Promise

The day surrenders, the sky ignites,
Stars awaken in soft delights.
A gentle breeze, a whispered call,
Night's embrace holds dreams for all.

As shadows dance, the world grows still,
With twilight's touch, hearts learn to fill.
In secret moments, hope takes flight,
Beneath the veil of soft moonlight.

Promises held in the starlit glow,
In silence shared, a love will grow.
For in the dusk, where stories flow,
A timeless bond, forever to know.

Shimmering Midsummer

Golden rays in the noonday sun,
Fields awaken, life's just begun.
Laughter dances on warm, soft air,
In every corner, joy is near.

With skies so blue, and flowers bright,
Nature sings in sweet delight.
The gentle hum of bees at play,
In summer's heart, we long to stay.

Barefoot wandering through fragrant fields,
In every moment, magic yields.
With each sunset, colors blend,
A shimmering promise, never to end.

Roots Beneath the Surface

Underneath, where shadows lie,
Roots entwine, as time slips by.
With silent strength, they anchor deep,
In hidden worlds, their secrets keep.

Beneath our feet, life intertwines,
Stories whispered in ancient lines.
From earth they draw, the strength to thrive,
In unity, they fight to live.

A tapestry of life concealed,
In every twist, the truth revealed.
For in the soil, our past connects,
Roots beneath, our hearts reflect.

Autumn's Embrace

Leaves of amber dance and sway,
Whispers of the cooler day.
Harvest moons in golden glow,
Nature's canvas, vibrant show.

Crisp air carries scents of spice,
Fields of pumpkins, all so nice.
Squirrels gather, nuts in tow,
As the fading sun moves slow.

Cider's warmth wraps us tight,
Fires crackle through the night.
Scarves and boots, our chilly gear,
Autumn's touch is ever near.

Beneath the boughs, we find our peace,
As the world begins to cease.
In this season's soft embrace,
Memories linger, time slows pace.

Golden hues in every glance,
Nature's beauty, a timeless dance.
As daylight fades, stars align,
Autumn whispers, "You are mine."

Winter's Candlelight

Snowflakes twirl in frosty air,
Laughter echoes everywhere.
Candleglow on window panes,
Warmth within the cold remains.

Blankets thick, the world's a hush,
Fires crackle, soft, and lush.
Sipping cocoa, joy abounds,
In this season, love surrounds.

Footprints mark the silent ground,
In each corner, magic found.
Carols sung by hearts alight,
Winter's charm, our pure delight.

Stars above in velvet night,
Shimmer softly, pure and bright.
Each moment wrapped in soft embrace,
Winter's wonder fills the space.

Glistening frosts on tree and lane,
Memories made without a strain.
In this season, hearts unite,
Winter's glow, our guiding light.

Summer's Sweet Serenade

Ocean waves kiss sandy shore,
Children laughing, spirits soar.
Sunshine paints the skies so blue,
Every moment feels brand new.

Picnics under shady trees,
Gentle whispers with the breeze.
Fireflies twinkle as stars play,
Longing for another day.

Ice cream drips on sun-kissed skin,
Barefoot dances, smiles within.
Evenings stretch with sunset gold,
In this warmth, our dreams unfold.

Beach bonfires, stories shared,
Memories made, laughter bared.
Freedom calls with every tide,
Summer's joy, we'll never hide.

Stars appear as darkness lays,
Nature hums her warm displays.
In summer's arms, we celebrate,
Life's sweet song, we recreate.

Vows in Bloom

Petals blush in morning light,
Promises that feel so right.
Two hearts dancing, hand in hand,
In this moment, life is planned.

Whispers soft, a gentle breeze,
Love blooms sweet among the trees.
Rings exchanged, our futures bright,
In each other, pure delight.

Laughter echoing through the air,
Every glimmer, every stare.
Vows like blossoms, fresh and true,
In this garden, me and you.

As the sun sets low and warm,
Heartbeats echo, safe from harm.
Together facing what's in store,
In this love, we'll find much more.

Branches sway, the world in tune,
Life together, sweet as June.
In this union, we are free,
Vows in bloom, just you and me.

Lanterns in the Night

In the quiet dark they glow,
Casting dreams where shadows flow.
Whispers soft, a gentle light,
Guiding hearts through endless night.

Beneath the stars, their warmth unfolds,
Stories shared, a bond that holds.
Each flicker tells a tale so bright,
Of hope and love, in the night.

Through the haze, their spirits rise,
Filling souls with sweet surprise.
Every spark a wish takes flight,
Lanterns dance, a pure delight.

In the sky, they drift like prayer,
Carried forth on midnight air.
Together, they illuminate,
The path of those who navigate.

They remind us, we are not alone,
In the darkness, seeds are sown.
With every glow, new dreams ignite,
Lanterns shine, our guiding light.

Twilight Declarations

As day turns to its gentle end,
Nature offers, time to mend.
Shadows stretch, embracing night,
In the dusk, our hopes take flight.

Voices whisper, soft and clear,
Promises made without a fear.
Each secret shared beneath the sky,
Twilight holds the reason why.

Colors blend in perfect grace,
Painting peace upon each face.
In this moment, hearts unite,
Underneath the fading light.

Silent vows that softly swell,
In our hearts, they weave their spell.
Declarations made with care,
Twilight's glow, a love we share.

As stars emerge, we hold the drift,
In twilight's arms, our spirits lift.
Every breath a step toward more,
With every sunset, we explore.

Threads of Connection

In the tapestry of life we weave,
Threads of connection, we believe.
Colors bright, entwined with chance,
In shared moments, we find our dance.

From heart to heart, a silent thread,
Binding words we've left unsaid.
In every laughter, every tear,
We discover what brings us near.

With open arms, we bring the light,
Shining bright through darkest night.
Threads of love, so strong and true,
In every bond, I find you.

Whispers shared, and stories learned,
In the warmth of love, hearts yearn.
Each moment held, a treasure found,
In life's fabric, we're tightly bound.

Together in this grand design,
Through every storm, we brightly shine.
Threads of connection, woven tight,
In the embrace of shared delight.

The Rhythm of Renewal

In the cycle of the moon's bright face,
Nature hums a sweet embrace.
With each dawn, we breathe anew,
The rhythm of life, the song so true.

Seasons change, the flowers bloom,
In the dance of life, dispelling gloom.
Every heartbeat sings a sound,
In this melody, we're unbound.

Through the struggles, we will rise,
Like the sun that paints the skies.
Each moment echoes, sweet and clear,
The rhythm of renewal draws us near.

With every step, we learn to grow,
In the dance of love, we come to know.
Life's embrace, a gentle guide,
In the rhythm, we walk side by side.

Embrace the ebb, accept the flow,
In this journey, let love show.
For in the music of our fate,
Is where we find our joy innate.

Love's Cycle Dance

In spring we bloom, soft whispers flow,
Hearts entwined as the warm winds blow.
A summer's kiss, bright and bold,
In every glance, sweet tales unfold.

As autumn leaves begin to fall,
We gather dreams, both great and small.
In twilight's glow, we find our way,
In love's embrace, we'll always stay.

Through winter's chill, our hearts remain,
A steadfast bond, like gentle rain.
In quiet nights, our laughter rings,
A symphony of love that sings.

With every turn, the seasons change,
Yet still our love, it feels so strange.
A cycle rich, forever dance,
In every moment, we find our chance.

Blossoms and Boughs

Underneath the cherry tree,
Petals fall so gracefully.
A blanket soft, a gentle ground,
Where love's true whispers can be found.

In fragrant blooms, we find our flight,
Colors bursting, pure delight.
With every breeze, a promise sings,
Of future hopes and cherished things.

The sturdy boughs, they hold us tight,
As shadows dance in fading light.
Together, we will sway and bend,
Embracing all that life can send.

Through seasons' change, the cycle bends,
Yet in our hearts, forever friends.
In every bloom, new dreams arise,
A garden nurtured under skies.

Winter's Embrace

Snowflakes fall like whispered dreams,
Blanketing the world in schemes.
The nights are long, the fires glow,
In winter's hush, our love will grow.

Each icy breath, a frosty kiss,
Moments shared that we won't miss.
In woolen wraps, we hold on tight,
Together through the starry night.

The silence deep, yet hearts ignite,
With every spark, we share the light.
Through frosted panes, the world is still,
Yet love's warmth is a potent thrill.

With every storm, we stand as one,
In winter's grip, our hearts weigh a ton.
In laughter and in cozy chats,
We find the joy in winter's mats.

Sunlit Promises

When dawn first breaks, the light does shine,
Awakening hope, a sign divine.
With every ray, our spirits lift,
In sunshine's glow, we share our gift.

The golden hours stretch so wide,
With warm embraces as our guide.
In playful dance, the shadows play,
As love ignites in bright array.

Across the meadows, laughter rings,
In sunlit moments, life's joy flings.
With every heartbeat, we begin,
A symphony where love's within.

Through dusky skies, our dreams take flight,
We soar together, hearts alight.
With promises beneath the sun,
In every heartbeat, we are one.

Staccato Heartbeats

In the silence, a rhythm found,
Echoing softly, a muted sound.
Quickened pulses call out to night,
A dance of shadows, bathed in light.

Every pause, a breath held tight,
Moments fleeting, taking flight.
Heartbeat racing, time compressed,
Life's tempo in a tangled fest.

Fleeting glances, sparks collide,
Emotions raw, no place to hide.
Staccato whispers, secrets shared,
In this chaos, hearts bared.

Counting beats, one after one,
Every throb a story spun.
In the night, we dare to dream,
Together, lost in the same stream.

When the music fades away,
Heartbeats linger, come what may.
In the end, we find our way,
With staccato hearts, we'll sway.

A Dance in the Rain

Raindrops falling, a gentle kiss,
Nature's rhythm, pure bliss.
Dancing lightly on the street,
The world sways to a heartbeat beat.

Umbrellas bloom like flowers bright,
Colors splashing, sheer delight.
Laughter echoes, spirits blend,
In the tempest, joy won't end.

Puddles shimmer, reflections swirl,
Feet twirling, visions unfurl.
Embracing storms, we lose our cares,
Every drop a dream that dares.

The sky weeps, yet we rejoice,
In the thunder, we find our voice.
With every step, life becomes clear,
In rain's embrace, there's nothing to fear.

As the clouds begin to part,
Sunlight breaks into our heart.
A dance in the rain, wild and free,
Together, forever, just you and me.

Whirlwind of Hues

Colors crash in a vibrant swirl,
Painting dreams in a vivid whirl.
Crimson skies and emerald fields,
Artistry of life, the world yields.

Brushstrokes bold, lines intertwine,
A mosaic of moments, divine.
Dappled sunlight, shadows blend,
In this canvas, hearts transcend.

Spectrum shifting, twilight dawns,
Gold and lavender, future spawns.
Nature's palette, a graceful dance,
Inviting all to take a chance.

In the whirlwind, we find our place,
Threads of joy, woven with grace.
Every shade tells a story bright,
In the chaos, we find light.

Whirling colors in the air,
Every hue a whispered prayer.
Together, we paint the perfect view,
In this whirlwind, love feels new.

Gentle Transitions

Morning light begins to break,
Softly whispering, a new wake.
The world turns, slowly awake,
Nature sighs for beauty's sake.

Day gives way to twilight's kiss,
In soft colors, we dwell in bliss.
Shadows stretch, the sun retreats,
In the quiet, longing beats.

Stars emerge, a twinkling choir,
Underneath the moon's soft fire.
Night embraces, a tender grace,
In dreams, we find our place.

Time flows softly like a stream,
In transitions, we truly dream.
Every moment, cherished, dear,
In gentle shifts, we persevere.

Seasons change, yet love remains,
Embracing joy, conquering pains.
In gentle transitions, hand in hand,
Together, forever, we stand.

Whirlwind Whispers

In the gusts they dance and sway,
Fleeting secrets lost to day.
Echoes of a stormy flight,
Whispers swirl in silver light.

Beyond the trees, the shadows play,
Carried forth on winds astray.
Voices murmur soft and low,
In the tempest's wild flow.

Glimmers flash, the skies ignite,
Nature's breath, a bold delight.
Thoughts entwined in stormy dreams,
Flow like rivers, swift and streams.

Fleeting moments like the breeze,
Gather near, then scatter free.
Let the whirlwind's heart be known,
In its chaos, find a home.

Each whisper holds a tale untold,
In the dance of winds so bold.
Listen close, the secrets find,
Stories weave through heart and mind.

Painted Horizons

Vistas stretch with colors bright,
Brushstrokes mingle, day and night.
Clouds like canvases unfold,
Whispers of a tale retold.

Shades of crimson, gold and blue,
Nature's beauty, ever new.
Sunset drapes like velvet cloth,
Embers dance as daylight sloth.

Mountains rise with peaks so grand,
Kissed by light from nature's hand.
Skyward dreams beyond the gray,
Hope takes flight in dusk's ballet.

Reflections in a tranquil stream,
Mirrored dreams, the world a dream.
Painted horizons, wide and free,
In every shade, eternity.

Beneath the sky, souls intertwine,
Artful whispers, soft divine.
Every sunset holds a start,
Colors warm the wandering heart.

The Timeless Tides

Waves of whispers kiss the shore,
Ancient songs the sea implores.
Rhythms echo, vast and wide,
In the dance of timeless tide.

Salt and spray, a fragrant air,
Footprints vanish, lost to stare.
Stories carve in grains of sand,
For a moment, hand in hand.

Moonlit paths on water's face,
Nature's pulse, a warm embrace.
In the depth, the secrets hide,
With the ebb and flow, we bide.

Every tide brings forth a tale,
Of journeys vast and hearts that sail.
Boundless dreams on ocean's swell,
Whispers of a world to tell.

Timeless tides, relentless beat,
In their arms, our hearts retreat.
Each wave a promise made anew,
In the sea's embrace, we grew.

Tapestry of Time

Threads of gold and silver shine,
Woven gently, fate aligns.
Moments stitched in subtle grace,
Stories dance in every space.

Yesterdays like shadows fade,
Memories in fabric laid.
Fading hues of laughter's past,
In the weave, our dreams are cast.

Weaving futures, bright and bold,
Stories yet to be retold.
Close your eyes, let visions flow,
In the loom, our spirits grow.

Time a tapestry unspooled,
With each thread, a lesson schooled.
Life's rich colors blend and sway,
In this art, we find our way.

Every strand a tale distinct,
In the fabric, hearts are inked.
Together, we embrace the climb,
In the endless tapestry of time.

Autumn's Palette

Golden leaves drift silently,
Crisp air whispers through the trees,
Nature dons her fiery robe,
A dance of colors in the breeze.

Pumpkin patches bask in sun,
Harvest moons glow through the night,
Footsteps crunch on fallen leaves,
As day gives way to soft twilight.

Fields of amber stretch for miles,
Squirrels scurry, gather, play,
Each moment savored slowly,
In autumn's warm, embracing sway.

Chilly mornings wrapped in fog,
Hot cider warms our weary hands,
While the world is painted bright,
In this season's tender strands.

As nights grow long and stars align,
We revel in the fleeting light,
Autumn's whispers, soft and clear,
A fleeting gift, a pure delight.

A Tapestry of Moments

Threads of laughter woven tight,
In the fabric of our days,
Every shared glance, every smile,
Each memory a golden blaze.

We dance through whispers of time,
Hand in hand, hearts open wide,
A tapestry of moments spun,
In the warmth of love's sweet tide.

Sunrise hopes, and sunset dreams,
Life's vibrant colors interlace,
In every heartbeat, every breath,
We find our strength, our rightful place.

Through challenges and quiet nights,
Our bond, a steady, shining thread,
Together we build our story strong,
In the tapestry where love is spread.

As seasons change, we will endure,
Each stitch a promise, each knot a vow,
In this journey, forever intertwined,
We weave our lives, here and now.

Love in Full Bloom

Petals unfold in morning light,
Soft whispers in the gentle breeze,
Hearts awash in colors bright,
Love's beauty brought to its knees.

Sun-kissed moments, sweet and pure,
Hands entwined on fragrant paths,
With every glance, a new allure,
In the garden of our soft laughs.

Time slows down where flowers sway,
Nature's canvas, vivid and wide,
Each bloom a promise, come what may,
Our sanctuary, love's safe guide.

Raindrops kiss the thirsty ground,
Nurturing dreams that gently rise,
In this place where hope is found,
Love blossoms under endless skies.

As petals fall, they leave their trace,
In the hearts that found their home,
Love in full bloom, our sacred space,
Together, never more to roam.

The Frosted Petal

Morning dew like diamonds shine,
Frosted petals glint in light,
Nature's art a quiet sign,
Of winter's kiss, soft and bright.

Brittle leaves whisper goodbyes,
To autumn's warmth, a fading glow,
Still beauty lingers, never lies,
In every flake, in every snow.

Hushed and still, the world takes pause,
A canvas dressed in white so pure,
Each frosty breath, nature's cause,
To create a beauty, crisp and sure.

Within the chill, a spark remains,
A promise forged in ice and bloom,
For spring will come to break the chains,
And chase away the winter's gloom.

So cherish all, the shifting tides,
Seasons turn, yet love will stay,
In the frost, the heart abides,
Waiting for the warmth of day.

Chasing Dawn

In the hush before the light,
Hope unfolds with every sight.
Whispers dance on morning's breath,
Life awakens, fears meet death.

Colors blend in soft embrace,
Chasing shadows, quickening pace.
As the sun begins to rise,
Dreams take flight, a new disguise.

Birds aloft in skies so clear,
Chirping tunes for all to hear.
Nature sings a vibrant song,
In this place, where hearts belong.

Morning dew on blades of grass,
Moments fleeting, time shall pass.
Yet within the golden glow,
Endless paths lie, waiting slow.

Light expands, the world awakes,
Every heartbeat, joy it makes.
Chasing dawn, we find our way,
Guided by the break of day.

The Canvas of Us

With every brushstroke we conspire,
To paint our dreams, ignite the fire.
Colors swirl in tangled bliss,
In every moment, find a kiss.

Vivid strokes of laughter bright,
Layered memories in pure delight.
Together we create the scene,
Life's a canvas, bold and keen.

Side by side, the world unfolds,
In vivid hues, our story told.
We build a masterpiece so grand,
With loving hearts and steady hands.

Pastels fade and shadows play,
Yet our colors never stray.
In every tear and every grin,
The canvas breathes, our love within.

Each day a stroke, each night a hue,
We blend the old with something new.
In the art of true romance,
We find the magic in our dance.

Shadows at Dusk

As daylight fades, the shadows creep,
Whispered secrets, silence deep.
Evening paints with darkened shades,
In twilight's arms, the world cascades.

Stars appear, a sprinkle bright,
Dancing dreams take flight at night.
The cool breeze carries tales untold,
In every breath, a heart of gold.

The horizon blushes, warm and shy,
Night ascends, the sun says goodbye.
In the shadows, lovers meet,
Their hearts entwined where darkness greets.

Moonlight casts its gentle glow,
Illuminating paths we know.
Through the night, we wander free,
Embracing all that's yet to be.

Underneath the velvet sky,
Whispers linger, a silent sigh.
In shadows at dusk, dreams unite,
A tranquil dance, the end of light.

Radiant Horizons

Where the sky meets ocean's sigh,
There, our spirits soar and fly.
Radiant colors, bold and brave,
Calling forth the dreams we crave.

With every step, the world expands,
Together we create new lands.
Horizons stretch beyond our view,
Every dawn a chance anew.

Cascading waves in rhythmic pulse,
Nature sings, we feel it vast.
With hearts aglow, we seek the path,
Embracing shadows, fleeing wrath.

Mountains rise against the skies,
With every challenge, we arise.
In the light of radiant hues,
We find strength in what we choose.

Adventure calls, our hearts aligned,
As we chase what's undefined.
Radiant horizons, we explore,
In every journey, we want more.

Tendrils of Connection

In the garden where we meet,
Whispers dance on summer heat.
Roots entwined, our spirits bloom,
Linking hearts in fragrant room.

Gentle breezes, soft and light,
Carry whispers through the night.
Tendrils stretch and intertwine,
In this space, your heart is mine.

Every glance that we exchange,
Brings the world a little change.
Silent vows in every sigh,
Bound together, you and I.

Through the trials and the joys,
We remain, two souls, one voice.
Grounded deep in love's embrace,
Finding strength in every space.

So as seasons ebb and flow,
Know our bond will only grow.
Hand in hand, we walk this way,
Tendrils tight, we'll never fray.

Layered Love

In layers soft, our love is formed,
Each one tender, gently warmed.
From surface shine to depths of soul,
Every fold makes us whole.

Underneath the quiet dreams,
Lie hidden hopes, or so it seems.
With every wrinkle, every crease,
Our hearts gather, finding peace.

Moments stitched with laughter bright,
Embroidered tales of day and night.
Binding threads of joy and tears,
We weave our story through the years.

In shadows deep and sunny rays,
Our layered love forever stays.
A tapestry of rich design,
With colors bold, our hearts entwine.

So let us cherish every seam,
And nurture this, our waking dream.
For in each layer lies the key,
To love that blooms eternally.

Underneath the Clouds

Beneath the cloak of weary gray,
Hope still stirs, it finds a way.
In between the drops that fall,
Resilience rises, standing tall.

Clouds may gather, filled with rain,
Yet through darkness, shines a grain.
A spark of light, a fleeting glow,
From below, our spirits grow.

Every storm brings fresh unrest,
But through the chaos, we are blessed.
For in the unseen, life abounds,
Underneath, our love surrounds.

Waiting patiently for dawn,
In whispered dreams, we carry on.
With every breath, together bold,
Our hearts are warmed, our stories told.

And when the clouds at last depart,
We'll share the rainbow with our heart.
Through storms we've walked, but still we stand,
Hand in hand, a faithful band.

Portrait of Promise

In hues of gold and shades of blue,
A portrait painted, me and you.
Each brushstroke tells a tale we've spun,
In this canvas, we're forever one.

Promises etched in colors bright,
Partners danced through day and night.
With every smile, a memory cast,
A bond unbroken, built to last.

Framed in laughter, shadows too,
Every corner holds a view.
Silhouettes of dreams we chase,
In this picture, time finds its place.

Hands together, strong and sure,
In every trial, love will endure.
Portraits fade, but love remains,
In our hearts, through joys and pains.

So let us paint, with colors bold,
Our future bright, as stories unfold.
In every stroke, a promise clear,
Together always, year after year.

Lovers' Seasons Turning

In springtime blooms, our love takes flight,
Petals drift softly, day turns to night.
Under blue skies, laughter fills the air,
Whispers of promises, sweet and rare.

Summer's embrace, the sun warms our skin,
In the golden glow, new dreams begin.
Dancing through twilight, hearts open wide,
Holding each other, nowhere to hide.

As fall descends, leaves whisper our tale,
Crisp air around us, we won't let it fade.
Crimson and gold like the love in our veins,
Every soft glance, like autumnal rains.

Winter arrives, a blanket of white,
In the stillness, our love burns bright.
With twinkling stars on a frosty night,
Together we'll weather each challenge in sight.

Seasons will change, yet we will remain,
Bound by the cycles, joy intertwined with pain.
Time's gentle passage, a dance we both know,
Through lovers' seasons, our hearts will inchoate flow.

Shadows and Sunbeams

In the twilight glow, shadows softly creep,
Echoes of laughter, memories we keep.
Golden sunbeams break through the trees,
A dance of light carried on the breeze.

Flickering moments, both dark and bright,
In the grand tapestry, we find our light.
Together we wander through valleys of shade,
A journey of growth, never afraid.

Clouds may gather, hiding the sun,
But still, our hearts beat as one.
We'll chase the horizon, where dreams take flight,
With shadows behind us, we'll soar to the light.

Among the uncertainties, warmth we will find,
In the gentle embrace of love so kind.
Navigating corners where doubts may loom,
Hand in hand, we'll brighten the gloom.

Shadows will whisper, but sunbeams will sing,
Every moment together, pure joy it brings.
Through shadows and sun, we'll journey anew,
In the canvas of life, just me and you.

The Kaleidoscope of Us

Twists and turns in a colorful frame,
Each time I look, I see something new.
Patterns evolving, reflections of love,
In this kaleidoscope, it's me and you.

Fragments of laughter, patches of tears,
Every color tells a story we share.
In the dance of life, we spin and we sway,
Creating a masterpiece, vibrant and rare.

Blue like the ocean, green like the trees,
Every hue whispers secrets of trust.
Through storms and sunshine, we'll always remain,
In this beautiful world, grounded like dust.

Radiant moments, a spectrum so bright,
Flashes of joy that light up our day.
Through shadows and changes, we will hold fast,
In this vivid embrace, come what may.

The kaleidoscope turns, and we find our way,
In the shifting forms, our spirits align.
What once was a puzzle, now seamlessly fits,
Forever together, your heart next to mine.

Embracing the Elements

The whispering winds carry stories untold,
Of earth and of fire, of warmth in the cold.
In the dance of the waves, the ocean's embrace,
We find the connection, a sacred place.

Lightning strikes bright, igniting the night,
In the heart of the storm, our love takes flight.
Through rain's gentle touch, we'll bathe in the glow,
With thunder as music, our spirits will flow.

Mountains stand tall, rooted in the ground,
Like our love, steadfast, forever profound.
In the embrace of the forest, beneath the broad sky,
Together we flourish, like birds soaring high.

Embers will flicker, yet never will fade,
Through every season, the bond we have made.
In the warmth of the fire, our passions ignite,
In the dance of the elements, everything feels right.

Nature's great symphony we both will adore,
In the heartbeat of life, we'll always explore.
Together we cherish the world as it turns,
Embracing the elements, forever it burns.

From Bud to Blossom

In the garden where dreams grow,
Tiny buds begin to show.
With whispers of the sun's sweet kiss,
They bloom to life, a moment's bliss.

Colors burst, a vibrant flare,
Petals dance upon the air.
Nature's brush paints with delight,
From soft dawn to gentle night.

Each flower tells a tale untold,
Of warm summers and winters cold.
They reach for skies, so wide, so vast,
A fleeting glimpse, then they pass.

In the breeze, sweet scents reside,
With every petal, joy and pride.
The cycle turns, it's time to grow,
From bud to bloom, a radiant show.

Seasons change, and still they stand,
Beauty crafted by nature's hand.
From silence comes a vibrant sound,
In every bloom, life's magic found.

Beneath the Canopy

In the woods where shadows play,
Leaves dance softly, sway all day.
Whispers echo, secrets shared,
In the depths, no soul is spared.

Sunlight filters, golden streams,
Mossy carpets cradle dreams.
Creatures scurry, life abounds,
In the quiet, heart's soft sounds.

Branches arch like open arms,
Sheltering all with nature's charms.
Beneath this vast and leafy dome,
The forest breathes, a sacred home.

Time stands still, in tranquil grace,
A hidden world, a sacred space.
Every rustle, every sigh,
Beneath the canopy, life draws nigh.

As twilight falls, the stars ignite,
In the hush, the world feels right.
The canopy, a starry sea,
Where dreams take flight, wild and free.

A Symphony of Seasons

Winter whispers with frosty breath,
Blanketing earth in quiet death.
Snowflakes dance in the pale moonlight,
A world transformed, so calm, so white.

Spring awakens with tender grace,
Life bursts forth, a warm embrace.
Blossoms paint the fields anew,
With colors bright, a vibrant hue.

Summer's laughter, a joyful tune,
Sunshine laughs beneath the noon.
Fields of gold, the harvest's cheer,
In every heart, warmth draws near.

Autumn sighs, in hues of fire,
Crimson leaves, a soft attire.
A bittersweet farewell it brings,
As nature hums her fading strings.

A symphony in every change,
Life's sweet rhythm, vast and strange.
In each season, beauty's found,
A dance of time, profound, unbound.

The Golden Hour

When daylight fades, the colors blend,
A painter's touch, time seems to bend.
Softest hues of orange and gold,
The golden hour, a sight to behold.

Shadows stretch, the world grows still,
Every heart knows the beauty's thrill.
Moments linger in twilight's glow,
As the sun dips low, the world slows down.

Birds take flight on whispered wings,
Nature sings of wondrous things.
In this hour, all worries cease,
A fleeting moment, purest peace.

Time stands still, embrace the light,
Chasing dreams into the night.
Every heartbeat, each breath profound,
In the golden hour, love is found.

So let us treasure these moments rare,
In the fading light, gentle and fair.
As day gives way to calm and deep,
In the golden hour, our souls will leap.

Melodies of Maturity

In the stillness, wisdom grows,
Lessons learned, in quiet flows.
Time, an artist, paints the past,
Molding futures, bright and vast.

With every note, the heart will sing,
Courage found in suffering.
A symphony of truth unfolds,
In every tale, a life retold.

In shadows cast, we find our light,
Embracing change, we take to flight.
Echoes linger, sweet and clear,
Melodies that draw us near.

From youthful dreams to elder grace,
Each moment holds a sacred place.
Harmony grows, with every scar,
Guiding us, our guiding star.

The Tapestry We Weave

Threads of color, bold and bright,
Intertwined, they dance in light.
Every choice, a strand unfurled,
Woven stories of our world.

Fingers trace the gentle lines,
Life's design in patterns shines.
Struggles, joys, a blend so rare,
Each thread holding love and care.

In every knot, a lesson learned,
From every tear, our passion burned.
Tapestry rich, in texture and hue,
Reflects the lives that we push through.

With every stitch, a memory made,
Rooted deep, they will not fade.
The fabric of us, strong and free,
In this design, our destiny.

Ebb and Flow

Waves of change, they rise and fall,
Guiding hearts through it all.
Moments rush like tides at sea,
Carving paths, setting us free.

Breezes whisper, secrets old,
In the depths, our truths are told.
With each push, we learn to swim,
In the currents, hope won't dim.

Flowing gently, time's embrace,
Instincts lead us to our place.
Ebb of doubt, the flow of trust,
In this journey, love is must.

Drifting softly, souls align,
In every storm, we find the sign.
Riding waves, both high and low,
Together, we learn to grow.

Whispers of Time

Time's embrace, a gentle sigh,
Moments flicker as they fly.
Whispers echo, soft and low,
Carrying dreams we long to know.

Fleeting shadows dance in light,
Memories linger, day turns night.
Each heartbeat, a timeless song,
Reminding us where we belong.

In silence, the past can speak,
Fragments of joy in the meek.
Every wrinkle, a tale concealed,
A legacy that's revealed.

What was lost can yet be found,
In every smile, love is crowned.
Whispers woven in our mind,
To cherish, to seek, to find.

Captured in Starlight

In the quiet of the night,
Stars twinkle bright and bold.
Whispers lost in silver light,
Secrets of the skies unfold.

Each twinkling gem above,
Tells a story yet untold.
Dreams take flight with hope and love,
In the arms of night so cold.

Glimmers dance upon the seas,
As the moonlight paints the shore.
Every heartbeat, every breeze,
Calls us back to moments more.

Captured in the starlit glow,
Time stands still, so sweet and clear.
In this world, we come to know,
Magic woven ever near.

Together under cosmic skies,
We forge paths with heart and mind.
In this place where wonder lies,
Eternal peace we hope to find.

In the Garden of Us

In the garden where we dream,
Petals fall like soft caress.
Every moment finds its theme,
Wrapped in love and tenderness.

Sunlight filters through the leaves,
Casting shadows, warm and light.
Each whisper of the breeze weaves,
A serenade in flight.

Blooming colors all around,
Nature's palette, pure and true.
In this space, our hearts are bound,
Every hue reflects me and you.

Butterflies dance, free and wild,
In this sanctuary of trust.
In our hearts, we are but children,
Finding joy in love, a must.

Together we tend paths of time,
Watering seeds, our dreams will grow.
Every challenge, every climb,
In the garden of us, we glow.

Hues of Heartstrings

Every color speaks to me,
In the twilight's soft embrace.
Hues of heartstrings, wild and free,
In this world, I find my place.

Scarlet echoes of my dreams,
Golden laughter in the air.
Azure skies hold whispered themes,
Every moment, every prayer.

Emerald coasts where memories lie,
Violet sunsets, time stands still.
Every heartbeat's gentle sigh,
Filling up this endless thrill.

Crimson shadows, midnight blue,
Paint a canvas wide and vast.
In this expanse, I find you,
Colors blend, our shadows cast.

Together crafting life's delight,
With every stroke, we redefine.
In the hues of starry night,
Love's pure essence, yours and mine.

The Timeless Arc

Beneath the dome of starlit skies,
Time unfurls her endless thread.
Moments weave, like whispered sighs,
In the stories left unsaid.

A river flows, a gentle grace,
Carving paths through hills and dreams.
In the silence, we find space,
To follow hope's unbroken beams.

Each chapter turns, a page revealed,
In the heart's eternal glow.
What was hidden now is healed,
In the dance of ebb and flow.

Hands held tight through dusk and dawn,
Marking time with every laugh.
Though the years may stretch and yawn,
Love endures as our photograph.

In this arc, we rise and fall,
Moments captured, never lost.
Together we can face it all,
For in love, we bear the cost.

Cradle of Starry Nights

Beneath the twinkling veil so high,
Whispers of dreams begin to sigh.
Moonlight dances on the trees,
Carrying secrets, sweet as breeze.

The night unfolds, a wondrous show,
A tapestry where starlight glows.
In every flicker, stories flow,
Of ancient tales and hearts that know.

Together we roam through celestial sea,
Hand in hand, just you and me.
The universe sings a lullaby,
Inviting us where shadows lie.

In the cradle of this night divine,
With you, my love, the stars align.
Every moment, a treasure to save,
In the embrace of the cosmic wave.

As dawn approaches, dreams take flight,
Yet in our hearts, we'll hold the night.
Forever marked by starlit grace,
We cherish every luminous trace.

Velvet Skies and Open Roads

Under the canopy of velvet hues,
The silent road whispers its cues.
We venture forth on paths untold,
Chasing horizons, brave and bold.

With every mile, the world transforms,
In laughter and love, our spirits warm.
Endless wonders beckon near,
In the journey, we find no fear.

The golden sun paints our way,
As we weave through night and day.
Each turn a promise, a memory to keep,
In the art of wandering, our hearts leap.

Among the stars, our stories blend,
In open roads, we find our mend.
A tapestry woven with every glance,
In velvet skies, we take our chance.

So here we stand, hand in hand,
In this fleeting moment, so grand.
With open hearts and endless skies,
Together we watch the horizon rise.

The Canvas of our Journey

Each step we take, a brushstroke made,
On the canvas where memories fade.
With every color, a tale unfolds,
Of laughter and love, of dreams that hold.

In shades of joy, our spirits soar,
Through valleys deep and mountains wore.
Every heartbeat, a vibrant hue,
In the masterpiece of me and you.

We wander through the fields of time,
In rhythm and rhyme, our lives align.
From dawn's soft glow to twilight's end,
In every glance, our souls transcend.

With brushes dipped in purest light,
We sketch our goals throughout the night.
In the gallery of what we've seen,
We dance on paths where dreams convene.

Together we stand, as artists true,
Creating a legacy, me and you.
In the canvas of our journey wide,
We'll paint our love, forever tied.

Love's Inclusive Palette

With every shade, our hearts conspire,
In love's embrace, we find our fire.
The whispers of colors softly play,
In this beautiful dance, we'll always stay.

From ruby reds to sapphire blue,
Each stroke a promise, binding two.
In the tapestry woven with threads of gold,
Lies the warmth of stories yet untold.

In the twilight's glow, our colors blend,
A spectrum of feelings that never end.
Through storms and sunlight, we remain bright,
Illuminating love, a shared delight.

With laughter and tears, we create the scene,
In an endless palette of what could have been.
Together we craft, together we dream,
In love's gentle rhythm, a perfect theme.

So let the canvas reflect our tale,
In every hue, let our hearts sail.
For love, my dear, is the art we choose,
A vibrant journey, forever infused.

Warmth in the Chill

Frosted breaths in morning's light,
Fireplace crackles, hearts take flight.
Wrapped in layers, snug and tight,
Whispers of warmth through the night.

Hot cocoa sips, laughter shared,
In this cozy nest, we're spared.
Outside, the world may cry and dare,
Inside, we find love and care.

Snowflakes dance as shadows play,
Each flake unique, bright as day.
In the beauty, we will stay,
Finding warmth in winter's gray.

Memories made, stories spun,
With every hug, our hearts are won.
Together, we bask in the sun,
So grateful for the chill that's done.

As seasons shift, new blooms will rise,
Yet in the cold, our bond complies.
Through every storm, our spirits fly,
For love remains, no need for sighs.

Evening's Serenade

The sun dips low, the sky ignites,
A canvas painted with gold lights.
Whispers of night begin to play,
An orchestra for the end of day.

Stars awaken, twinkling bright,
Cool breezes dance with sheer delight.
Moonlit shadows gently sway,
Where melodies of heartstrings lay.

Crickets sing their soothing tune,
Settling under the watchful moon.
A symphony of nature's grace,
Time slows down in this sacred space.

Reflections spark in twilight's haze,
Memories blend in the evening's gaze.
As the world finds its soft embrace,
Harmony thrives in love's warm place.

In every note, a promise sweet,
As drumbeats echo beneath our feet.
Together we sway, hearts in sync,
Forever bound, in evening's wink.

Seasons of Surrender

Autumn leaves in colors bold,
Whispers of stories yet untold.
Nature sheds its summer gown,
Preparing for winter's soft brown.

Frosty mornings greet the day,
With whispers of the winds that play.
Snowflakes drift on silent air,
A world transformed, precious and rare.

Spring awakens, life anew,
Flowers bloom in every hue.
Tender shoots break through the ground,
In vibrant promises, joys abound.

Summer's heat, a blazing fire,
Days grow long, our spirits higher.
Golden sunsets paint the sky,
In every moment, dreams can fly.

In this dance of time we find,
Life's a journey, intertwined.
Through all seasons, peace is near,
In surrender, love casts fear.

A Journey Through Time

Footsteps echo on dusty roads,
Maps of memories etched in codes.
Moments linger, weaving tales,
In the heart where time prevails.

Worn-out faces and aged hands,
Each line a story, life expands.
Through laughter, joy, and sometimes tears,
Together we face all our fears.

Pages turn as seasons blend,
Snapshots gathered, memories lend.
In every heartbeat, history flows,
Binding us in what truly grows.

The clock ticks on, relentless stride,
Yet in our hearts, we'll always bide.
In every second, love's sweet rhyme,
Our souls entwined through endless time.

To journey forth, with open eyes,
Finding wonder in the skies.
In every moment, life will shine,
A beautiful dance, a journey divine.

Tangled in Time

Moments slip through fingers, slow,
Like grains of sand in a glass.
Whispers echo in the wind,
As shadows of the past amass.

Memories weave a tapestry bright,
Stitched with laughter, hope, and tears.
In the silence of the night,
We find solace from our fears.

Time, a river, flows and bends,
Carrying dreams and distant sighs.
A journey where all paths blend,
With every heartbeat, life complies.

Yet in the moments, we must stand,
To grasp the beauty that we find.
For in our hearts, we understand,
The value of the ties that bind.

So let us dance through fleeting hours,
Embrace each second, swift and bright.
For tangled in time's gentle flowers,
We bloom together, day and night.

Gardens of Gratitude

In the garden where we grow,
Seeds of kindness take their flight.
With every dawn, the flowers glow,
A canvas painted with delight.

Raindrops fall like silver stones,
Quenching earth with soft embrace.
Among the roots, our hearts have grown,
In gratitude, we find our place.

Leaves whisper stories of the past,
Their rustling filled with gentle cheer.
In every moment, memories last,
As petals dance, our truths appear.

Sunshine spills its golden rays,
Kissing blooms with warmth and grace.
In this haven, time decays,
As love entwines in every space.

So let us tend this sacred land,
Watered by the joys we share.
With open hearts, we take a stand,
In gardens of gratitude, we care.

Waves of Togetherness

Tides roll in, a rhythmic song,
Embracing shores with tender grace.
Together, we have lived so long,
In the ocean's warm embrace.

With every wave, a story told,
Of laughter, love, and dreams at sea.
In currents deep, we find the bold,
Our spirits dancing, wild and free.

Sunset casts a golden sheen,
As we walk hand in hand along.
In that moment, pure and keen,
The horizon sings our shared song.

The moonlight guides our paths anew,
Stars twinkle like our hopes and fears.
In the depths, I find in you,
A bond that time will not unsear.

So let the waves crash, let them roar,
In unity, we shall remain.
For together, we are evermore,
Bound by love, entwined in gain.

A Chorus of Intertwined Lives

Voices rise like gentle streams,
Weaving tales of joy and strife.
In the chorus of shared dreams,
    Harmony adorns our life.

Each note carries a history,
A thread connecting heart to heart.
In the symphony, we see,
    How every soul plays a part.

Through trials faced and laughter shared,
    Our melodies, both sweet and true.
In love's embrace, we are repaired,
    Every whisper, a bond anew.

Together we create a song,
With verses rich and bridges wide.
A testament where we belong,
    In unity, we shall abide.

So let us rise in joyful sound,
As notes of life begin to flow.
In the chorus, we have found,
The beauty in the seeds we sow.

The Stillness Between

In quiet moments, time holds breath,
We find our thoughts in soft caress.
The world outside fades from our sight,
In stillness, we discover light.

Silent whispers paint the night,
Linking hearts with gentle might.
The space we share, a sacred zone,
In silence, love has truly grown.

Between the noise, we hear our song,
A melody where we belong.
With every pause, we feel the beat,
In stillness, life feels pure and sweet.

Eyes to eyes, the language flows,
In this moment, the universe glows.
Pausing here, we breathe as one,
In stillness, the journey's just begun.

Together wrapped in twilight's grace,
In this stillness, we find our place.
The warmth of you, a guiding star,
In timeless space, we've traveled far.

Crisp Pages of Our Story

Fingers trace the lines we wrote,
A tale alive, a heartfelt note.
With every turn, new dreams ignite,
In pages crisp, our souls take flight.

Moments captured, laughter shared,
In the ink, our truths laid bare.
Each chapter holds a piece of time,
In perfect rhythm, we start to climb.

Through storms and sun, our words entwine,
Stories woven, yours and mine.
With every line, a spark appears,
In the pages, we fight our fears.

Tales of joy and whispered pain,
In each record, we rise again.
Crisp pages turn, a fragrant breeze,
In every word, our hearts find ease.

Together we'll pen, through night and day,
In inked love, we'll find our way.
The story grows, with every sigh,
In these crisp pages, we learn to fly.

Playful Shadows

In the golden light, we dance and sway,
Casting shadows in a playful way.
Each movement brings a story to life,
In patterns bright, we find our strife.

Laughter echoes through the air,
As shadows mingle, free from care.
With every leap, a shadow flicks,
In playful dreams, time gently ticks.

Underneath the vibrant skies,
We chase the light, where freedom lies.
Memories stretch and blend with grace,
In shadows, we embrace our place.

The world alive with hues so bold,
In twilight's glow, adventures unfold.
Through every frame, our hearts align,
And in those shadows, we'll intertwine.

With every dusk, our joys increase,
As shadows dance, we find our peace.
In each embrace, we feel the thrill,
In playful shadows, time stands still.

Echoes of Change

In the winds of time, whispers call,
Echoes of change, a soft enthrall.
With every breeze, new paths emerge,
In the sound of life, we find the urge.

Casting worries to the sea,
Embracing all that's meant to be.
The rhythm shifts, the leaves all sway,
In echoes loud, we learn to play.

Through seasons bright, and shadows deep,
In every heart, a promise keeps.
Transformation sings, a tender tune,
In echoes of love, we find the moon.

New horizons greet our eyes,
As change unfolds, we rise and rise.
In this journey, we search for light,
In every echo, our spirits ignite.

Embracing paths we've yet to tread,
In echoes, we're forever led.
With every step, a chance to grow,
In echoes of change, our spirits flow.

Weaving Through Time

Threads of past entwine with dreams,
In shadows long, as daylight seems.
A tapestry of moments bright,
Each stitch a whisper, lost in light.

Memories dance on a silken loom,
Carried forth to dispel the gloom.
Fingers trace the stories spun,
In every hue, a life begun.

Woven paths through ancient skies,
Connecting hearts with unseen ties.
The echoes call, a gentle prime,
In every heartbeat, weaving time.

Seasons change, the threads unfold,
New patterns form, both bright and bold.
Yet still the past resides within,
In woven tales, our lives begin.

Through every twist, the fabric glows,
A vibrant life, as the river flows.
In every fiber, dreams entwine,
In the great loom, we weave through time.

Embracing Change

The winds of change begin to blow,
A soft embrace, a gentle flow.
In shifting tides, we learn to bend,
And in each start, we find an end.

Branches sway beneath the sky,
Letting go, as moments fly.
Through every turn, an open door,
In learning loss, we gain much more.

Seeds take root in fertile earth,
From darndled soil, arises birth.
With every change, we grow anew,
In colors bright, we chase the blue.

The river flows to carve its way,
In every twist, a new array.
A dance of shadows, light and dark,
In moments fleeting, we leave our mark.

As seasons shift, we learn to trust,
In every trial, a bond of rust.
Embracing all that life will bring,
In every change, our spirits sing.

Puddles of Reflection

Raindrops fall on cobblestone,
Each gentle splash, a world alone.
In puddles deep, our dreams float high,
Mirroring hopes beneath the sky.

Faces change in rippled light,
Fragments captured, lost from sight.
In silent depths, the past does gleam,
Reflecting softly what we dream.

A moment's pause to catch the view,
In each reflection, something new.
Stories swirl like autumn leaves,
In tiny pools, our heart believes.

Colors blend in liquid dance,
Like fleeting love or happenstance.
In every drop, a truth resides,
Where whispers linger, hope abides.

As sun breaks through the cloudy dome,
The puddles shine, and hearts find home.
In every spark, the world refracts,
In puddles deep, we find our tracks.

The Language of Leaves

Whispers rustle through the trees,
In every motion, a gentle breeze.
Leaves converse in hues of green,
A language shared, yet seldom seen.

Each flutter carries tales untold,
Of seasons past and marigold.
In sunlight's kiss, a story weaves,
In silence deep, the heart receives.

Branches reach to touch the sky,
While roots dive deep, where secrets lie.
Leaves fall softly, a golden rain,
In every whisper, joy and pain.

Amidst the dance of shade and light,
Nature's voice speaks day and night.
In every color, a truth revealed,
In the language of leaves, we're healed.

Through autumn's chill, they'll bid goodbye,
Yet promise life beneath the sky.
In every rustle, hope remains,
In the language of leaves, love sustains.

Whispers of the Wedded Wheel

In the quiet night, vows softly shared,
Beneath the stars, two hearts bared.
Promises woven in silver light,
Together they dance, in love's delight.

With laughter that echoes, hands entwined,
In this sacred bond, the soul aligned.
Through trials faced, and joys embraced,
Their journey begun, no time is misplaced.

As seasons change, so do they grow,
In every whisper, love's gentle glow.
In each heartbeat, a story spun,
Forever they travel, two as one.

With dreams held close, they chase the dawn,
In the garden of life, their love is drawn.
Through storms they weather, in peace they find,
In every moment, their spirits aligned.

Together they forge a path anew,
In every glance, a love so true.
With each step taken, they know the thrill,
Of whispers exchanged on the wedded wheel.

Tides of Togetherness

Upon the shore, hand in hand,
The tides pull back, and then expand.
Waves of laughter crash and play,
In the sun's embrace, they drift away.

With gentle whispers, secrets shared,
A bond so strong, no one has dared.
In the ocean's arms, their spirits rise,
Together they soar, beneath vast skies.

As the moonlight dances on the sea,
They find their rhythm, wild and free.
Each tide a promise, deep and wide,
In this journey, love's faithful guide.

In quiet moments, they pause and reflect,
On the beauty found in each sweet connect.
With hearts like anchors, they hold on tight,
In the glowing dusk, their souls take flight.

Through the ebb and flow, they'll navigate,
In the tides of togetherness, they find fate.
With every wave, a story unfolds,
A timeless tale of love retold.

Radiance of Resilient Roses

In a garden bright, the roses bloom,
Each petal whispers, dispelling gloom.
With colors bold, they sway and dance,
Resilience shines in every chance.

Through storms they withstand, roots held tight,
In the darkest hours, they find the light.
With fragrance sweet, they draw you near,
A testament of love, crystal clear.

Every thorn tells a tale of pain,
Yet beauty flourishes, like gentle rain.
In the sun's warm kiss, they reach for skies,
The radiance glows in nature's eyes.

As seasons shift, they fade and grow,
In the cycle of life, wisdom flows.
With each new bloom, a hope, a dream,
Together they thrive, a vibrant theme.

In gardens tended with loving care,
Resilient roses, a bond so rare.
With every breath of fragrant air,
The power of love is found everywhere.

Springtime Promises

As winter fades, new life will spring,
In every bud, a song they sing.
With colors bright, the earth awakens,
In every heartbeat, hope is taken.

With gentle rains, the seeds take flight,
In golden sun, all feels so right.
Through whispered breezes, joy arrives,
In spring's embrace, the spirit thrives.

The days grow longer, the light is warm,
In every moment, love's the charm.
Filled with laughter, the world takes part,
In the canvas of life, they paint their heart.

Among the blooms, they laugh and play,
With hands held close, they greet the day.
Promises whispered with each soft breeze,
In the magic of spring, they find their ease.

Together they walk, through fields of dreams,
In the warmth of love, life brightly beams.
With every sunrise, their spirits soar,
In springtime promises, forevermore.

Echoes of Laughter

In the quiet of the night,
Whispers of joy take flight.
Memories dance in the air,
A melody sweet and rare.

Footsteps of childhood play,
Chasing the clouds of the day.
Each giggle, a gentle spark,
Lighting the world from the dark.

Time moves in a soft embrace,
Echoes linger, a warm trace.
We gather 'round, hearts unite,
In laughter, the world feels right.

With friends, we weave our tales,
On journeys where love prevails.
In moments both small and grand,
Together, we take a stand.

May laughter forever flow,
A river where dreams can grow.
In the heart's enchanting glow,
Echoes of joy will bestow.

Harvest of Dreams

In fields where hopes arise,
Seeds of vision touch the skies.
Each yearning, a fragrant bloom,
Filling our lives, dispelling gloom.

Together we plant and sow,
Watering thoughts as they grow.
The sun shines bright, paths aglow,
In this garden, dreams overflow.

Moonlit nights whisper our fate,
Under the stars, we contemplate.
Caught in the thrill of the chase,
Each dream a vibrant embrace.

The fruits of our labors thrive,
In the heart, we come alive.
With every rise of dawn's gleam,
We cherish this harvest of dreams.

With every laughter and scream,
We gather the joys that redeem.
In every moment, love beams,
In the light of our shared dreams.

Shades of Togetherness

In hues of soft twilight,
We gather, hearts shining bright.
Each shade tells a different tale,
Woven bonds will never pale.

Through rain and sun, storm and calm,
Together we stand, a soothing balm.
Hand in hand through thick and thin,
In this dance, we find our kin.

Colors blend in perfect grace,
Creating a warm, safe space.
The laughter shared, the tears shed,
In love's embrace, we are led.

Every shade, a memory dear,
Echoing hope, banishing fear.
In these moments, we find peace,
Together, our joys increase.

As dawn breaks with vibrant light,
We cherish each shared insight.
In the canvas of our days,
Shades of togetherness always stays.

A Kaleidoscope of Us

In the mirror of our days,
Colors dance in wondrous ways.
Each moment a vibrant hue,
Reflecting the love that's true.

Twists and turns, we explore,
Life's patterns, forever more.
In this magic, joy unfolds,
A tapestry of heart and souls.

With laughter, we paint the night,
In swirling shades, hearts take flight.
Embracing change with open arms,
Each new turn brings fresh charms.

Through trials that test our might,
We find strength in shared light.
A kaleidoscope, vibrant and bold,
Tales of love and hope retold.

As we journey, hand in hand,
Each color helps us understand.
In the beauty that we trust,
Forever shines the kaleidoscope of us.

Echoes of Eternal Affection

Whispers in the quiet night,
Hearts entwined, a gentle light.
Memories softly intertwine,
Love's sweet echo, pure and fine.

Through the shadows, spirits dance,
Each glance held a fleeting chance.
In the silence, feelings grow,
Softly, tenderly, they flow.

A timeless bond, forever strong,
In each heartbeat, we belong.
Across the years, we find our way,
Guided by love's soft array.

Fading twilight, dreams take flight,
Wrapped in warmth, you feel so right.
Two souls merge, a sacred space,
Marked by love's sweet, warm embrace.

An echo sings of days gone by,
In laughter shared, we reach the sky.
Eternal whispers in the night,
Together still, our hearts take flight.

Harvest of Hearts

In fields where golden grains do sway,
We gather love at end of day.
Each moment shines, like sunlit gold,
A treasure far more than wealth untold.

With every laugh, seeds we sow,
In tenderness, our bounty grows.
Hands entwined, the work takes flight,
Together forging day and night.

The fruits of trust, in laughter found,
In softest whispers, love unbound.
A harvest rich with joy's embrace,
In every heart, we find our place.

As seasons change, our bond will last,
Through every storm, through shadows cast.
We reap the joy of every hour,
In the garden of love, we bloom and flower.

From roots of hope, our dreams arise,
Like summer stars in twilight skies.
Each heartbeat sings a timeless tune,
In the harvest of hearts, love's boon.

Chasing Morning Dew

As dawn breaks softly, shadows flee,
We chase the dew, just you and me.
Each drop a promise, fresh and new,
A dance of light, in morning's hue.

With laughter ringing in the breeze,
We feel the rush of nature's tease.
In every sparkle, dreams unite,
Two souls awakened in pure delight.

The world is bright, our spirits high,
As sunlight spills across the sky.
With every step, we feel so free,
In harmony, just you and me.

Through fields of green, we wander far,
With hearts ablaze like a shooting star.
Chasing the dew, we find our way,
In the glow of a brand new day.

In fleeting moments, time stands still,
With every breath, a joyous thrill.
Together chasing, hearts aglow,
In the morning light, love will flow.

Sunlit Moments

In sunlit moments, laughter rings,
A symphony that joyfully sings.
With every smile, the world ignites,
Embraced by warmth of golden lights.

We dance through fields of wildflowers,
Bathed in sunshine's gentle showers.
A tapestry of day's delight,
With you, my heart takes its flight.

Time slips by like flowing streams,
In every gaze, we weave our dreams.
Sunset whispers, soft and low,
Together wrapped in evening's glow.

With every heartbeat, love expands,
As we walk through these vibrant lands.
Moments cherished, take our breath,
In the beauty of life, we find depth.

So here we stand, in light we trust,
In sunlit moments, love is a must.
Forever glowing, side by side,
In every heartbeat, love abides.

Frost-kissed Reveries

The morning light begins to gleam,
Frosty whispers in a dreamy scheme.
Each crystal spark, a tale untold,
Nature's quiet wonders unfold.

Silent trees draped in white lace,
A gentle breath in this tranquil space.
Footprints crunch on a path so pure,
In this serene, we feel secure.

Birds flit by in the azure sky,
As winter's magic begins to fly.
Moments freeze in a breathtaking sight,
Wrapped in warmth, in soft twilight.

A cup of cocoa, warmth in hand,
Gazing out at the frosty land.
Heartfelt wishes on a chilly breeze,
In frosted dreams, we drift with ease.

So let the chill enhance the glow,
In quiet paths where wonders flow.
Through winter's grace, we find our song,
In frost-kissed nights, we all belong.

Sweethearts in Cycle

A dance of hearts beneath the moon,
Each gentle glance, a quiet tune.
Two souls entwined in the softest light,
Sweethearts thrive in the warmth of night.

Seasons change, yet love holds true,
Through stormy skies and skies of blue.
Hand in hand, they wade through time,
With whispered dreams, their hearts align.

Cherry blossoms fall in spring's embrace,
Promises bloom in every place.
With each passing day, their roots grow deep,
In tender moments, their love they keep.

Through summer's heat, they chase the day,
In laughter bright, they weave their play.
Under starlit skies, they make a vow,
In love's sweet dance, they find their now.

As autumn leaves begin to sway,
Their love stands tall, come what may.
In every cycle, their bond will last,
For hearts like theirs are unsurpassed.

Petals of Time

Time flows softly like a gentle stream,
Moments woven in a silken dream.
Petals fall, as seasons pass,
Memories cradle, forever vast.

Spring blooms bright, colors alive,
Nature's canvas helps us thrive.
In every petal, stories freeze,
A dance of life, a breeze with ease.

In summer's glow, laughter rings,
Joy takes flight on youthful wings.
Joyful days drift like a song,
Embracing all where hearts belong.

Autumn whispers, leaves cascade,
The tapestry of life is laid.
Golden hues tell of days gone by,
As twilight calls with a gentle sigh.

Winter wraps the world in white,
Time takes pause in the quiet night.
Yet even in the chill we find,
The warmth of love forever binds.

The Dance of Changing Days

The sun awakes with golden rays,
Igniting skies where beauty plays.
In every dawn, a promise blooms,
Each moment whispers, life resumes.

Clouds drift lazily, softly glide,
Embracing change like the rising tide.
In vibrant hues, the hours dance,
Life unfolds in its wild romance.

Birds take flight in morning's grace,
Chasing shadows that time can trace.
Eyes to the horizon, dreams ignite,
As possibilities stretch into light.

Evening falls, the world slows down,
Stars awaken, the moon wears her crown.
In twilight's embrace, we pause and see,
The beauty of change, where we are free.

Through every season, day by day,
In the dance of time, we find our way.
With every step, new tales arise,
In the changing dance, love never dies.